A Study Guide

for

CELEBRATION
OF DISCIPLINE

A Study Guide

for

CELEBRATION OF DISCIPLINE

Richard J. Foster

HODDER AND STOUGHTON

LONDON   SYDNEY   AUCKLAND   TORONTO

British Library Cataloguing in Publication Data

Foster, Richard, *1946–*
    A study guide for Celebration of Discipline.
    1. Society of friends—Prayer-books and devotions
    I. Title
    242   BV4501.2

    ISBN 0-340-32989-0

Hodder and Stoughton Editorial Office: 47 Bedford Square, London WC1B 3DP

To Ken and Doris Boyce

Who believed in me and encouraged me and filled a
great void within me when the lives of my own
parents were cut short

CONTENTS

ABOUT THIS STUDY GUIDE

If I rightly understand the function of a study guide, it has two goals. First, it is to make the issues raised in the book even more pointed and specific. Second, it is to enlarge and further the discussion of the book. As you can quickly see, these two goals are virtual opposites. One tries to nail things down, the other tries to open things up; one tries to narrow the discussion, the other tries to broaden the discussion. But both tasks are essential in any genuine learning situation.

The brief essays at the beginning of each chapter are usually aimed at broadening and expanding the landscape of the Discipline. This is especially true with the introductory chapter in which I attempt to expose to your view the foundation upon which the Spiritual Disciplines are built. In a couple of the essays I do try to clarify several items mentioned in the book.

Each essay is followed by Scripture passages for personal or group study. It is of utmost importance that we flesh out our understanding of the Spiritual Disciplines in light of the Bible, for it is our sure foundation in all matters of faith and practice.

It is important for you to understand the function of the study questions. While some of the questions are aimed at helping you to read the book carefully (that is, they fulfil the first goal of making the isssues clear), the majority of the questions are meant to encourage an expanded understanding of the Spiritual Disciplines. The questions do not have in mind answers that are a foregone conclusion. They are not intended to elicit parrot-like recall but to encourage thought and discussion. In this I have kept in mind the perceptive comment of John Ciardi, "A good question is never answered. It is not a bolt to be tightened into place but a seed to be planted and to bear more seed toward the hope of greening the landscape of ideas."

Obviously the bibliographies are provided in the hope that you will become sufficiently drawn into the subject so that further exploration becomes necessary. The books provide guidance for your journey. I have attempted to include a good variety, from literature for the beginner to the more advanced. Hopefully, the annotations will guide you to those books which will meet your specific needs. For each chapter I have included several of the recognized classics in the field.

It is my hope that this study guide might serve in some small way to enhance your ability to be attentive to the voice of the true Shepherd. If these words (which are a broken and fragmentary witness at best) can point you to Jesus Christ, your ever-living ever-present Teacher, they will have served their purpose.

Richard J. Foster
Friends University
March 1982

Introduction

THE GOOD LIFE

It is one thing to praise discipline, and another to submit to it.
— Don Quixote de La Mancha

If we expect to enter wholeheartedly into the experience of the Spiritual Disciplines we must understand clearly that they are meant to open us to the Good Life.* Their purpose is not to make life miserable but joyful, not to put us in bondage but to set us free, not to confine but to liberate.

There is a general cultural confusion today about the Good Life; and, given the popular notion of abundance, it is almost impossible to believe that God is good and that His desire is to fill our lives with His goodness. In the modern world the Good Life is often identified with power, wealth, status and freedom from all authority. We have today two systems of teaching about the abundant life that are diametrically opposed to one another. The one system has its roots in the culture around us; the other has its roots in the God of Abraham, Isaac, and Jacob. Both claim to bring us into the Good Life, and we must underscore the fact that their teachings are mutually exclusive. We will never see the classical Disciplines of the spiritual life as a good thing until we perceive their function of bringing us into the abundant life of the Kingdom of God. And we cannot see this until we

---

*It was my friend, Dr Dallas Willard, Associate Professor of Philosophy at the University of Southern California, who first helped me to see the connection between the Spiritual Disciplines and the classical discussions of the Good Life. I owe a great debt to him in helping me to understand what makes life abundant, through both his teaching and his life.

are able to understand how life under God and in His Kingdom is truly good and ultimately fulfilling, as opposed to the "good life" of human invention.

In the Bible we see that God desires to give us a full life, and that abundance consists in the proper correlation of three things: provision, place and personality. Human life is such that goodness consists of a combination of these three.

Provision

Provision involves all things necessary to carry on human life adequately. God intends that we should have enough to meet our needs. In human society there is misery from a simple lack of provision — witness the immense suffering of many in the Third World. Christianity is the most materialistic of the world's religions: that is, it takes material things seriously as created goods God has given us to enjoy.

The Old Testament is saturated with promise after promise of provision, "The Lord your God will bless you in all your produce, and in all the work of your hands, so that you will be altogether joyful" (Deut. 16:15). Note that the rejoicing is because of the abundant provision from the hand of God. The New Testament picks up this same theme of God's care for those who trust in Him. Jesus makes it unmistakably clear that all those who seek first His Kingdom and His righteousness have all of the provision necessary for a happy life. We will be more adequately cared for than the lilies of the field.

On the other hand, we must beware of how people have taken the teaching on provision and twisted it into a thing of their own. It has been turned into a religion of personal peace and prosperity, crudely stated, "Love Jesus and get rich". However, it is also incarnated in much more subtle but equally destructive forms. And the interesting thing about all these formulas for blessedness is that they work; that is, they work if what we want is a little money. But if we desire the abundant life of the Kingdom of God – a life filled with holiness and free of avarice – they fail miserably.

What we need to see is that provision is a limited good, limited in the sense that we cannot make a life out of it. The moment we make a life out of provision, we deify it and lose the spiritual grace of contentment. We must never deny the fact that provision is good, but we must always understand that it is a limited good.

I should add that within the concept of provision is the adequate provision of time. People whose lives are fractured and fragmented cannot know abundance. There needs to be adequate time for reflection, meditation, rest, conversation. The reasons many of us do not have the timeful life are varied, but the root problem is that we are not living in the Christian grace of simplicity. It is easy to see that the Spiritual Disciplines of meditation, solitude and simplicity are dealing in large part with the concept of provision.

Place

Place is the second element essential to the Good Life. Place is a *mutually understood* and *accepted* set of personal relationships which give identity to the life. When I say that place must be "mutually understood", I mean that everyone involved needs to have the same expectation level of an individual's place. When I use the word "accepted" I mean that it should be viewed as a good thing. (It is very common today to view place as bad.)

Obviously place is more a social function than it is a location. When we speak of refugees as "displaced persons", we mean more than that they have had to leave their homes; we mean that all their roots have been torn up, their sense of identity as persons badly shaken.

Scripture has a great deal to say about place. In the Old Testament world there was a place for the aged, the widowed, the orphan. Today there is less real place for them in the mainstream of human society. (The Church today is struggling to find place for the divorced, and that single struggle accounts for an immense amount of grief in contemporary society.)

The New Testament describes the Church as a set of places. The apostle Paul is describing the place of the various members of the body of Christ when he discusses the Spiritual Gifts. There is a place, a proper function, for the apostle, the prophet, the evangelist, the teaching pastor, and all the gifts of the Spirit. The Epistles include quite sensitive and sensible descriptions of the place of the husband and wife, the parent and child, the slave and master. In our day some people have horribly misunderstood these instructions and have used them to manipulate and control other human beings. Others, deeply fearful of the stereotypes which have been given to place, have rejected the concept of place altogether. Neither group has understood the teaching of Scripture and both end in misery.

We must understand that there is simply no abundant life apart from place. That goes down very hard today, especially among people who have felt oppressed by their place (and we should reject oppressive places), but we cannot be placeless. As long as we are finite we must have a sense of place, a role, a function.

You can quickly see that the Spiritual Disciplines of submission, service and guidance deal with the question of place.

Personality

The third element that needs to be integrated into human life for there to be abundance could be called personality. Personality refers to the inward person, expressed in certain determinate ways or ingrained habits. Right here is the main problem for many of us. We have ingrained habits that defeat us over and over again. It is at the level of ingrained habits that the main work of redemption occurs so far as the transformation of our lives is concerned. If we are going to experience the Good Life, certain deeply embedded habits are required. Conversely, to have an abundant life there are certain ingrained habits from which we need to be liberated. Since our slavery occurs mainly at the habit level, our freedom is discovered primarily at this level. In short, I am speaking of power, power from God which enters the life and transforms the habit patterns.

Jesus diagnosed the apostle Peter's problem this way: "The spirit indeed is willing, but the flesh is weak" (Mt. 26:41). That graphically depicts the situation for many of us – we want to do what is right but we seem to be unable to do so. But Jesus Christ did not intend that problem to continue for Peter, nor does He intend that it should continue for us. In Scripture we are instructed on how the flesh can be brought into a working harmony with the spirit in obedience to the ways of God and in the context of contemporary life.

But this reality is not found in some four easy steps to blessedness – or even in twelve easy steps! It involves a voluntarily accepted and consciously chosen course of action that includes both individual and group life which will set us before God in such a way that He can produce the needed change. As you can see, the major burden of *Celebration of Discipline* is to describe this process and to show how the personality can be transformed by the power of the Holy Spirit. It is a practical manual on sanctification.

The Failure of Law and Ritual

All of us are aware of the fact that we fall short of this grand vision of God's goodness for our lives. In a frantic scramble to experience adequate provision, we succumb to the golden calf of materialism. Then in an attempt to exorcise the consumer demon, we cut back in such a way that we threaten the family's viability and the children's hopes for college education. Or we determine to understand who we are – our sense of identity, our sense of place – but in the process develop inner habit patterns of egoism and downright arrogance. Or, perhaps, we begin to see victory over the ingrained habit of gluttony only to discover an inner pattern of anger come bubbling to the surface. And the moment we think we are holding everything in line, the deep-seated patterns of pride cloud the entire landscape.

Human sin is written across the face of humanity. It is very real to us all and only serves to show our difficulties in entering into the Good Life of the Kingdom of God.

From the beginning, men and women have sought to free themselves from this crushing human predicament. The normal means for solving our dilemma have been law and ritual. Either we set up a series of laws which we hope will cover every situation or we devise religious rituals. (It matters little which we use – High Church types usually tend toward ritual, Low Church types toward law – they are in reality two sides to the same coin.) Neither of these, of course, succeeds in transforming the human personality though, as Jesus mentioned, they often make quite nice-looking whitened sepulchres. Usually these are accomplished by a heavy exertion of the will, but the effort is doomed to failure. Paul Tournier writes, "To depend on one's own will-power, one's good resolutions, especially against the impulsions of instinct and the determinism of powerful, psychological complexes, is to ask for failure and for a perpetual conflict which will destroy rather than strengthen the forces of the person."

There is a proper place for the will, but it is not in transforming the inner person. The will functions in the *decision* to place our lives before God so that He may work within us; as the old Spiritual puts it, "I have decided to follow Jesus." And that decision is a continual one, for the following of Jesus is continual. The will plays an important part in the function of the Disciplines, but we are never made righteous by exertions of the will. Righteousness is a gift from God, that comes as we place ourselves before Him.

The function of the Spiritual Disciplines is now clear. They are *means* for receiving God's grace. God's desire is to bring us into that way of living in which our needs are cared for, our sense of identity as individuals is clarified, and the inward life becomes whole and unified. To this end Jesus Christ lived, died, was resurrected, and ever lives to be our present Prophet, Priest, and King. The salvation that is in Christ involves not only the forgiveness of sins and heaven when we die, but the breaking of the power of sin so that we can live in newness of life now.

The Good Life of the Kingdom of God breaks into our hearts by the grace of God alone. We are not only saved by grace but live by it as well. However, we must see (and this is essential if we are to avoid the ancient heresy of antinomianism) that we have a part to play in the drama of holiness. To be sure, it is only a bit part in a huge pageant but it is an essential one. Our work – our only work – is to place ourselves in the way of Christ and invite Him to work in our lives individually and corporately. The Spiritual Disciplines are merely an attempt to describe how that is done. They sketch out (surely only in part) the means of grace whereby we are placed before God. Having done this, the Disciplines have reached the end of their tether. Beyond this no human being can go. The change is God's work, and as it comes we sing joyfully, "Amazing grace, how sweet the sound, that saved a wretch like me".

Daily Scripture Readings

What modern thinkers call "The Good Life" the Biblical writers would identify as "The Godly Life" and our understanding is immeasurably deepened by studying scriptural examples of those who come to walk in the joy of the Lord.

Sunday   – Jesus Christ: the *Summum bonum* of the Good Life.
           All four gospels beginning with Mark

Monday   — The example of Abraham. Genesis 12–25

Tuesday   — The example of Elijah. I Kings 17–19, II Kings 1–2

Wednesday — The example of David. I Samuel 16–27, II Samuel 1–12, 22–23:7

Thursday   — The example of Daniel. Daniel 1–12

Friday   — The example of Peter. The gospels, Acts 1–5, 10–11. (See also his epistles)

Saturday   — The example of Paul. Acts 9, 11–28. (See also his epistles)

Suggestions for Further Reading

There is nothing that gives content to the Good Life and fleshes out the meaning of our own spirituality quite like reading the Saints throughout the ages. They lift our spirits, free us from the cult of the contemporary, and give us models to imitate.

Anderson, Courtney, *To the Golden Shore: The Life of Adoniram Judson*, Grand Rapids: Zondervan Publishing Co., 1977. (The moving story of the man who through great suffering burned the gospel into the heart of Burma.)

Brainerd, David, *The Life and Diary of David Brainerd*, ed. Jonathan Edwards, Chicago: Moody Press, 1980. (In this fine book Jonathan Edwards is able to reconstruct the inward conflicts and struggles of the soul of this godly pioneer missionary to the North American Indians.)

Brother Ugolini di Monte Santos, *The Little Flowers of St Francis*, trans. Raphael Brown, Garden City: Image Books, 1958. (Stories of early Franciscans which will delight, shock and challenge you.)

The Confessions of Saint Augustine, trans. Edward B. Pusey, D.D., New York: Collier Books. (The intense spiritual search by the man destined to become one of the major figures in Christian history.)

Fitts, A.P., *The Life of D.L. Moody*, Chicago: Moody Press, 1979. (The story of the evangelist who dared to see what God would do with a man totally committed to Him.)

Fox, George, *The Journal of George Fox*, ed. John Nickalls, New York: Cambridge University Press, 1952. (The first of the modern journals which set the standard for the many which would follow, including the more famous *Journal of John Wesley*. Written by the major figure of seventeenth-century Quakerism, it is filled with power and vigour.)

Grubb, Norman, *Rees Howells Intercessor*, Guildford: Lutterworth Press. (The story of the Welshman who made prayer the most notable feature of his life.)

Journals of Jim Elliott, ed. Elizabeth Elliot, Old Tappan: Fleming H. Revell, 1978. (The powerful journal writings of one of the five men martyred by the Inca Indians at the middle of the century.)

Julian of Norwich, *Showings*, trans. Edmund Colledge, O.S.A. and James Walsh, S.J., London: S.P.C.K., 1979. (Sixteen "Showings" or revelations of God's love which came to Julian in a series of visions. A fourteenth-century English mystic, her revelations of the feminine side of God are of particular interest today.

Madame Guyon, *Madame Guyon: An Autobiography*, Cambridge: James Clark Co. Ltd., 1961. (This well-known seventeenth-century mystic wrote this introspective account of her life while in prison for her faith.)

Merton, Thomas, *The Seven Storey Mountain*, London: Sheldon Press, 1978. (The early days of the twentieth century's most famous trappist monk. See also Monica Furlong's excellent *Merton: A Biography*, Collins (William), Sons & Co. Ltd., 1980.)

Müller, George, *Autobiography of George Müller*, ed. H. Lincoln Wayland, Grand Rapids: Baker Book House, 1981. (In his own words the story of the man who interpreted for us the meaning of faith through his large orphanages and other Christian work which he financed and sustained through prayer alone.)

Pascal's Pensées, trans. W.F. Trotter, New York: Collier, 1960. (Terse statements on life and faith by the acclaimed scientist, inventor, psychologist, philosopher and Christian apologist of seventeenth-century France.)

Sadhu Sundar Singh, *At The Master's Feet*, trans. Rev. Arthur and Mrs Parker, Old Tappan: Revell Company, 1922. (Moving words on the life of faith by "the Saint Paul of India". You may also want to read the powerful story of Sundar's life, *Sadhu Sundar Singh* by Cyril J. Davey, STL Books, 1980.)

Seaver, George, *David Livingstone: His Life and Letters*, New York: Harper and Brothers, 1957. (The moving story of Livingstone's pioneer work in Africa both in evangelism and in efforts to abolish the slave trade.)

Sheen, Fulton J., *Treasure in Clay: The Autobiography of Fulton J. Sheen*, New York: Doubleday, 1980. (An intimate autobiography by the archbishop who became so well known to Americans through his radio broadcasts and later his television series.)

Taylor, Dr and Mrs Howard, *J. Hudson Taylor: A Biography*, London: Hodder & Stoughton Ltd., 1973. (The story of the man who opened inland China to the gospel and learned to walk in faith in exceptional ways.)

Walker, F. Deauville, *William Carey: Father of Modern Missions*, Chicago: Moody Press, 1980. (The life of the man who called the world to "Expect great things from God! Attempt great things for God!")

Wesley, John, *The Journal of John Wesley*, ed. Percy Livingstone Parker, Chicago: Moody Press, 1951. (The journal record of the man who boldly said, "The world is my parish" and who founded the Methodist movement.)

Woolman, John, *The Journal and Major Essays of John Woolman*, ed. Phillips P. Moulton, New York: Oxford Press, 1971. (In terms of the issues which it addresses – racism, war and peace, faith in God, etc. – this is the most contemporary of all the journals in my opinion.)

Chapter 1

THE SPIRITUAL DISCIPLINES: DOOR TO LIBERATION

As you begin this study of the Christian Disciplines, there are several pitfalls that advance warning may help you to avoid. Briefly, I shall list seven – surely there are more!

The first pitfall is the temptation to turn the Disciplines into law. There is nothing like legalism to choke the heart and soul out of walking with God. The rigid person is not the disciplined person. Rigidity is the most certain sign that the Disciplines have gone to seed. The disciplined person can do what needs to be done when it needs to be done. The disciplined person can live in the appropriateness of the hour. The disciplined person can respond to the movings of divine grace like a floating balloon. Always remember that the Disciplines are perceptions into life, not regulations for controlling life.

The second pitfall is the failure to understand the social implications of the Disciplines. These are not a set of pious exercises for the devout, but a trumpet call to obedient living in a sin-racked world. They call us to wage peace in a world obsessed with war, to plead for justice in a world plagued with inequity, to stand with the poor and disinherited in a world that has forgotten its neighbour.

A third pitfall is to view the Disciplines as virtuous in themselves. In and of themselves the Disciplines have no virtue, possess no righteousness, contain no rectitude. It was this important truth that the Pharisees failed to see. The

Disciplines place us before God; they do not give us Brownie points with God.

A fourth and similar pitfall is to centre on the Disciplines rather than on Christ. The Disciplines are for the purpose of realizing a greater good. And that greater good is Christ Himself, who must always remain the focus of our attention and the end of our quest.

A fifth pitfall is the tendency to isolate and elevate one Discipline to the exclusion or neglect of the others. The Disciplines are like the fruit of the Spirit – they comprise a single reality. Sometimes we become intrigued with fasting, for example, and we begin to think of that single Discipline as comprising the whole picture. What is only one tree we see as the whole forest. This danger must be avoided at all costs. The Disciplines of the spiritual life are an organic unity, a single path.

The sixth pitfall is to think that the twelve Disciplines mentioned in *Celebration* somehow exhaust the means of God's grace. I have no exhaustive list of the Christian Disciplines and as far as I know none exists, for who can confine the Spirit of God? *Celebration* is merely one attempt to compile those acts of devotion which the writers of Scripture and the Saints throughout the history of the Church have said were important in experiential faith. But Christ is greater than any attempt to describe His workings with His children. He cannot be confined to any system, no matter how worthy.

The seventh pitfall is the most dangerous. It is the temptation to study the Disciplines without experiencing them. To discuss the Disciplines in the abstract, to argue and debate their nature or validity – these we can do in comparative safety. But to step out into experience, this threatens us at the core of our being. And yet there is no other way. Prayerfully, slowly, perhaps with many fears and questions, we need to move into this adventurous life of the Spirit.

Daily Scripture Readings

Sunday   – The longing to go deeper. Psalm 42

Monday   – The slavery to ingrained habits. Psalm 51

Tuesday   – The slavery to ingrained habits. Romans 7:13–25

Wednesday – The bankruptcy of outward righteousness. Philippians 3:1–16

Thursday   – Sin in the bodily members. Proverbs 6:16–19

Friday   – Sin in the bodily members. Romans 6:5–14

Saturday   – The victory of Spiritual Discipline. Ephesians 6:10–20

Study Questions

1. I say that "Superficiality is the curse of our age." If you tend to agree list several indicators in our culture that would illustrate this fact. If you tend to disagree list several indicators in society that would illustrate your conviction. Are there influences in our day that would cause Christian people to be more superficial than Christian folk of other centuries?

2. I refer to the Disciplines discussed in this book as "classical". What reason do I give for saying this? Critique my rationals – that is, do you agree or disagree?

3. What is the purpose of the Spiritual Disciplines?

4. What is a primary requirement to embarking on this journey? Are there things that would keep you from fulfilling this requirement?

5. Consider carefully Heini Arnold's statement, "We want to make it quite clear that we cannot free and purify our own heart by exerting our own will". Does that ring true in your own experience?

6. I indicate that those who desire to explore the world of the Spiritual Disciplines are faced with two difficulties. What is the "practical difficulty"? Can this be seen in your own life? What is the "philosophical difficulty"? How can this be seen in your own life?

7. What do I mean by "disciplined grace"? What does the concept of "cheap grace" mean? With which of these two types of grace are you most familiar?

8. If you were walking on the narrow ledge of which I speak, which side would you fall from most often? Explain how this can be seen in your own life.

9. As you read the book, consider what you feel are the most dangerous things about the book. (That is, what elements might lead people away from God, rather than to God?)

10. What struck you most forcefully in this chapter? Were there areas you disagreed with, or were unable to identify with, or perhaps found difficult to understand?

Suggestions for Further Reading

There is a wealth of literature on the Spiritual Disciplines, and the following represent some of the best works in the general field of the spiritual life. They provide an excellent background and framework out of which to study the Christian Disciplines.

Arnold, Heini, *Freedom From Sinful Thoughts*, New York: Plough Publishing House, 1973. (A book full of insights on inner thought by a leader in the Hutterian Society of Brothers.)

Bonhoeffer, Dietrich, *The Cost of Disciplieship*, London: S.C.M. Press, 1964. (The book which gave us the term "cheap grace" and which so forcefully called us to a more costly form of discipleship.)

Brother Lawrence, *The Practice of the Presence of God*, trans. E.M. Blaiklock, London: Hodder & Stoughton Ltd., 1981. (These simple letters and conversations by Nicholas Herman – Brother Lawrence – of France have inspired three centuries of Christians to live in more intimate communion with Christ.)

Day, Albert Edward, *Discipline and Discovery*, Tennessee: The Upper Room, 1977. (A manual written especially for the "Disciplined Order of Christ" but containing practical wisdom for us all.)

Fénelon, François, *Christian Perfection*, Harper & Row, Inc., Minneapolis: Dimension Books, 1975. (Letters of spiritual counsel and direction on a multitude of practical matters by the French Archbishop who advised numerous individuals in the court of Louis XIV. Other recent editions of his writings include *The Royal Way of the Cross* and *Let Go*.)

Francis de Sales, *Introduction to the Devout Life*, London: Scholar Press, 1976. (Much of this material is the result of counsel Francis gave to a single individual, Mme Louise Charmoisy, in the early seventeenth century. It covers a wide variety of spiritual matters for those seeking to deepen their devotional life.)

Freer, Harold Wiley, *Christian Disciplines*, New York: Pageant Press, Inc., 1960. (Short meditations which show an unusual awareness of the Devotional Classics.)

Jean-Pierre de Caussade, *The Sacrament of the Present Moment*, San Francisco: Harper & Row, Publishers, Inc., 1982. (Written by an eighteenth-century French Jesuit; it is sheer delight to read.)

Kelly, Thomas R., *A Testament of Devotion*, London: Quaker Home Service 1979. (I can count on one hand the twentieth-century classics of devotion – this is one of them.)

Kempis, Thomas À., *The Imitation of Christ*, trans. E.M. Blaiklock, London: Hodder & Stoughton Ltd., 1979. (A new translation by E.M. Blaiklock adds fresh vitality to this undisputed leader of the classics of Christian devotion.)

Law, William, *A Serious Call To A Devout and Holy Life*, ed. Paul G. Stanwood. London: Dent (J.M.) & Sons Ltd., 1979. (An influential work on the Christian life by the person often called the greatest of the post-Reformation English mystics. Law was the leader of a small spiritual community and included among his disciples John and Charles Wesley.)

Nee, Watchman, *The Normal Christian Life*, Eastbourne: Victory Press, 1971. (An important statement on the Christian life which stands in counter-distinction to so much of "normal Christianity".)

Nouwen, Henri J.M., *Making All Things New*, Dublin: Gill & Macmillan Ltd., 1982. (A small but powerful invitation to the spiritual life centring on the Disciplines of solitude and community.)

O'Connor, Elisabeth, *Journey Inward, Journey Outward*, New York: Harper & Row, Publishers, Inc., 1968. (More than a continuation of the story begun in *Call To Commitment*, it sets forth the twin disciplines of the inward journey of devotion and the outward journey of service.)

Peterson, Eugene H., *A Long Obedience in the Same Direction*, Downers Grove: InterVarsity Press, 1980. (Through a study of the "Songs of Ascents" – Psalms 120–134 – Eugene Peterson helps Christians wrestle with many of the classical Spiritual Disciplines.)

Sanford, Agnes, *The Healing Light*, Evesham: James (Arthur) Ltd., 1981. (The classic statement on the healing ministry to which Jesus calls the Church and a book which has influenced my own pilgrimage immensely.)

Taylor, Richard Shelley, *The Disciplined Life*, Minnesota: Beacon Hill Press, 1962. (A sharp plea for disciplined living in an age of self-indulgence.)

Tozer, A.W., *The Pursuit of God*, Bromley, Kent: S.T.L. Books, 1980. (A tender, sensitive book filled with insight and a catholicity of outlook that is refreshing.)

Anthologies of Devotional Classics

An Anthology of Devotional Literature, ed. Thomas S. Kepler, Grand
    Rapids: Baker Book House, 1977. (Contains selections of many of
    the important Christian writers from Clement of Rome to Karl
    Barth.)

The Doubleday Devotional Classics, ed. Glenn Hinson, 3 vols, New
    York: Doubleday, 1978. (Contains a wide variety of choice
    specimens from the vast treasury of Protestant spirituality.)

Living Selections From the Great Devotional Classics, Nashville: The
    Upper Room (various dates), (twenty-nine booklets that are
    available as a set or individually. An excellent way to introduce
    people to some of the best of the devotional writers.)

Chapter 2

THE DISCIPLINE OF MEDITATION

The purpose of meditation is to enable us to hear God more clearly. Meditation is listening, sensing, heeding the life and light of Christ. This comes right to the heart of our faith. The life that pleases God is not a set of religious duties; it is to hear His voice and obey His word. Meditation opens the door to this way of living. Jean-Pierre de Caussade wrote, "There remains one single duty. It is to keep one's gaze fixed on the master one has chosen and to be constantly listening so as to understand and hear and immediately obey his will."

Meditation is a more passive Discipline. It is characterised more by reflecting than by studying, more by listening than by thinking, more by releasing than by grabbing. In the Discipline of meditation we are not so much acting as we are opening ourselves to be acted upon. We invite the Holy Spirit to come and work within us – teaching, cleansing, comforting, rebuking. We also surround ourselves with the strong light of Christ to protect us from any influence not of God.

Since some have asked, I might just as well come clean and tell you that I have *no* interest at all, or experience, in astro-travel or any of the other rather exotic forms of meditation. Perhaps that reflects my own prejudice but such approaches, it seems to me, do not resonate well with the biblical witness. I find little ethical content or concern for moral transformation in these forms of meditation. I am much more interested in the kind of hearing that Abraham,

Moses and Elijah knew, which brought forth a radical obedience to the one true God.

In *Celebration* I gave only a brief description of the meditation upon Scripture, assuming that people were quite familiar with this form of meditation. In this assumption I was wrong, and so I should like here to provide a brief meditation upon John 6 as an example of one approach to the *meditatio Scripturarum*. It is my hope that this will encourage all of us to drink deeply and extensively at this, the most central and important form of Christian meditation.

The story is a familiar one – Jesus' feeding of the five thousand. Begin by imagining yourself the child who gave his lunch, or perhaps the child's parents: at any rate, try to place yourself in the actual scene. Following the counsel of Ignatius of Loyola, attempt to use all of the senses as you slowly read the passage. Try to see the story – the grass, the hills, the faces of the people. Try to hear the story – the sound of the water, the noise of the children, the voice of the Master. Try to feel the story – the texture of your clothing, the hardness of the ground, the coarseness of your hands. Finally, try to feel with your emotions – hesitancy at bringing your lunch, astonishment at the miracle of multiplied food, joy at the gracious provision of God. At first this approach may necessitate several readings of the text.

Then in your imagination watch the crowd leave and Jesus go up into the hills. You are left alone. You sit on a rock overlooking the water re-experiencing the events of the day. You become quiet, and after a little while Jesus returns and sits on a nearby rock. For a time you are both silent, looking out over the water perhaps, and enjoying one another's presence. After a bit, the Lord turns to you and asks this question, "What may I do for you?" Then you tell Him what is in your heart – your needs, your fears, your hopes. If weeping or other emotions come, do not hinder them.

When you have finished, you become quiet for a little while. Then you turn to the Lord and ask, "What may I do for you?" And then you listen with the heart quietly, prayerfully. No instruction needs to come, for you are just glad to be in Christ's presence. If some word does come to you, take it with utmost seriousness. More often than not, it will be some utterly practical instruction about seemingly trivial matters, for God wants us to live out our spirituality in the ordinary events of our days. And I have often found them to be wonderful words of life. What I have shared here is, of course, only an example – God will, I am sure, give you many other ways to enter into the life of Scripture.

Beyond this, may I make a plea for the memorization of Scripture.* Through memorization the biblical witness becomes rooted deep in the inner mind and begins to mould and adjust our world view almost without our realizing it. Then too, as we submit ourselves to this small discipline, God is able to teach us through the word of Scripture at any given moment, even in sleep. It is a helpful means to enhance our meditation upon Scripture.

Daily Scripture Readings

Sunday   – The glory of meditation. Exodus 24:15–18

Monday   – The friendship of meditation. Exodus 33:11

Tuesday   – The terror of meditation. Exodus 20:18–19

Wednesday – The object of meditation. Psalm 1:1–3

Thursday   – The comfort of meditation. I Kings 19:9–18

Friday   – The insights of meditation. Acts 10:9–20

Saturday   – The ecstasy of meditation. II Corinthians 12:1–4

*Contrary to popular myth, memorization is quite easy once one catches onto the idea. The Navigators have published numerous aids which make the task even more possible.

Study Questions

1. What are some of your first reactions to the idea of meditation? What is your background experience in this area?

2. What is the basic difference between Eastern meditation and Christian meditation?

3. What are some of the things that make your life crowded? Do you think you have a desire to hear the Lord's voice in the midst of all the clutter?

4. Experience the following words of Frederick W. Faber for fifteen minutes. Record what you learn from the experience.

> Only to sit and think of God,
>   Oh what a joy it is!
> To think the thought, to breathe the Name
>   Earth has no higher bliss.

5. What threatens you most about meditation?

6. What do you think about dreams as a means of hearing from God? Have you had any experience in this area?

7. List the five forms for meditation which I give. Ponder the fifth form and what it might mean today given the contemporary political scene.

8. What do you see as the value of thinking through the specifics of time, place and position in regard to the experience of meditation?

9. What are the dangers in concentrating on time, place and position?

10. Do "Palms down, Palms up" today. Note anything you learn about yourself.

Suggestions for Further Reading

Brother Lawrence, and Frank Laubach, *Practicing His Presence*, ed. Gene Edwards, Goleta: Christian Books, 1981. (A helpful bringing together of selections from *Letters by a Modern Mystic* and *The Game With Minutes* by Laubach and a modern rewrite of Lawrence's famous *The Practice of the Presence of God*.)

Downing, Jim, *Meditation: The Bible Tells You How*, Colorado Springs: NavPress, 1976. (A practical little book by a leader among the Navagators on the active side of meditation upon Scripture.)

Kelsey, Morton T., *The Other Side of Silence*, London: S.P.C.K., 1977. (The most important single book on the theology and psychology behind the experience of Christian meditation.)

Merton, Thomas, *Contemplative Prayer*, London: Darton, Longman & Todd Ltd., 1973. (A powerful analysis of the central nature of contemplative prayer. A must book.)

Merton, Thomas, *Spiritual Direction and Meditation*, Wheathampstead: Clarke (Anthony) Books, 1975. (Written mainly with the monastic life in mind but filled with a discernment and practical wisdom which all can appreciate.)

Moffatt, Doris, *Christian Meditation: The Better Way*, New York: Christian Herald Books, 1979. (Simple meaningful prayer techniques and specific meditations that will help the beginner move forward into Christian meditation.)

O'Connor, Elizabeth, *Search For Silence*, Waco: Word Books, 1972. (Brings into focus the art of quietness and contemplation through meaningful exercises and a wealth of quotations from the devotional masters.)

Russell, Marjorie, *A Handbook of Christian Meditation*, Old Greenwich: Devin-Adair Company, 1978. (A practical, clear guide to the actual methods of meditation.)

Tilmann, Klemens, *The Practice of Meditation*, London: Search Press Ltd., 1977. (A handbook on Christian meditation which draws on both Eastern and Western tradition. The last third of the book has numerous meditations upon Scripture.)

Chapter 3

THE DISCIPLINE OF PRAYER

As I travel I find several common misconceptions that defeat the work of prayer.

The first misconception is the notion that prayer mainly involves asking things from God. Answers to prayer are wonderful, but they are only secondary to the main function of prayer, which is a growing perpetual communion. To sink down into the light of Christ and become comfortable in that posture, to sing "He walks with me and He talks with me" and know it as a radiant reality, to discover God in all of the moments of our days and to be pleased rather than perturbed at the discovery – this is the stuff of prayer. It is out of this refreshing life of communion that answered prayer comes as a happy by-product.

The second misconception is to view prayer as always a struggle, "getting under the burden of prayer", as we say. I certainly would not want to deny those times of intensity and difficulty, but I have not found that to be the most common experience. Nor would I want to minimize the sense of awe and even terror which we feel in the presence of the Sovereign of the universe. And yet, the most frequent experience is one of lightness, joy, comfort, serenity. Even laughter comes at times, though it is richer and less pretentious (should I say more holy) than ordinary laughing. There is a feeling of companionship, though again it is of a different quality from the ordinary human variety. Perhaps it is that we are becoming the friend of God.

A third misconception is that we live in a closed universe, that everything is fixed. We think, "Since everything is set and God knows the end from the beginning, why pray?" The question is a good one. Perhaps you have had the frustrating experience of talking with an employer about some company policy being considered for adoption. Your employer may invite you to share your concerns and seems to listen intently. Then later you discover that the decision had already been made long before you ever entered the room. Many folk feel that way about prayer. But if the apostle Paul is right that "we are God's fellow workers" (I Cor. 3:9), then ours is indeed an open universe. We are working with God to determine the outcome of things. It needs to be said reverently, but it does need to be said – we are co-creators with God in advancing His kingdom upon the earth.

A fourth misconception is the fear that our faith will crumble if our prayers are not answered the first time, every time. As one person put it to me, "If God doesn't answer this prayer, it is all over; I will never be able to believe in prayer again." It is this fear that causes us to gravitate toward vague prayers – then if nothing happens no one is the wiser. But suppose I walk into my office and turn on the light switch and nothing happens. Would I say, "Well, I never believed in electricity anyway!" No, I would assume something is wrong, and I would set out to find out what it is: perhaps the bulb is burned out or the connection is faulty. The same is true with prayer, and very often I have found the problem is indeed a faulty connection at our end.

A fifth misconception about prayer is the common teaching, "Pray once! Any more than that shows a lack of faith." Now I understand the good intentions of people who teach this way but, very frankly, it flies in the face of a great deal of biblical experience and teaching, especially Jesus' parables of importunity. We are to keep at this work, mainly I think because we are the channel through which God's life and light flows into individuals or situations. And, incidentally, I have found prayer to be the most helpful of the Disciplines in freeing us from the monsters of the past because of the inner healing that comes through the hands of those who pray for us.

May I call you to the adventure of prayer – nothing draws us closer to the heart of God.

Daily Scripture Readings

Sunday – The pattern of prayer. Matthew 6:5–15

Monday – The prayer of worship. Psalm 103

Tuesday – The prayer of repentance. Psalm 51

Wednesday – The prayer of thanksgiving. Psalm 150

Thursday – The prayer of guidance. Matthew 26:36–46

Friday – The prayer of faith. James 5:13–18

Saturday – The prayer of command. Mark 9:14–29

Study Questions

1. Why do I say, "To pray is to change?" Have you ever experienced that in your own life?

2. How can we keep from being discouraged by the example of the "giants of the faith"?

3. What difference would it make in our praying to believe that we live in an "open universe" or a "closed universe"?

4. Why is it important to view prayer as a learning process?

5. Distinguish between the prayer of faith and the prayer of guidance.

6. Frank Laubach said, "I want to learn how to live so that to see someone is to pray for them." Take up that experiment for one whole day and record what you learn from the experience.

7. What is your response to the idea of using the imagination in the work of prayer?

8. *Look* at someone today and imagine what they could be if they received a double portion of the light of Christ. By faith give it to them and record what you learn from the experience.

9. What should we do when we don't feel like praying?

10. What experience have you had of the Thomas Kelly statement on page 40?

Suggestions for Further Reading

Bounds, E.M., *Power Through Prayer*, Grand Rapids: Zondervan Publishing House, 1979. (This stimulating call to the ministry of prayer was written primarily to preachers but provides plenty of challenge for all who dare to read it.)

Grou, Jean Nicholas, *How To Pray*, trans. Joseph Dalby, Cambridge: Clarke (James) & Co. Ltd., 1955. (This book by a French Jesuit of the eighteenth century is, in the words of Evelyn Underhill, "One of the best short expositions of the essence of prayer which has ever been written.")

Hallesby, Ole, *Prayer*, Leicester: Inter-varsity Press, 1961. (Written by one of Norway's leading devotional writers, this book is aimed at helping the average Christian develop a more meaningful life of prayer.)

Kimmel, Jo, *Steps To Prayer Power*, New York: Abingdon Press, 1972. (A brief, practical, and genuinely helpful guide to prayer.)

Laubach, Frank C., *Prayer: The Mightiest Force in the World*, Old Tappan: Fleming H. Revell Co., 1959. (A book born out of the practice and zeal of one of the truly great missionaries of the twentieth century who was often called "the apostle of literacy".)

Leech, Kenneth, *True Prayer*, London: Sheldon Press, 1980. (Henri Nouwen said it well, "*True Prayer* not only speaks about prayer, but it creates the space in the reader where prayer can grow and mature.")

Murray, Andrew, *With Christ In The School Of Prayer*, Old Tappan: Fleming H. Revell Co., 1970. (A grand classic dealing with the ministry of intercession by a great preacher and pray-er of the last century.)

Nee, Watchman, *The Prayer Ministry of the Church*, Hollis: Christian Fellowship Publishers, Inc., 1973. (More likely than not this book will disturb you and challenge many of your cherished ideas about prayer and as a result force you to think and experience more deeply the work of prayer.)

Sanders, J. Oswald, *Prayer Power Unlimited*, London: Lakeland Paperbacks, 1978. (Practical guide to personal prayer with useful discussion questions at the end of each chapter.)

Theresa of Avila, *The Interior Castle*, trans. Kieran Kavanaugh and Otilio Rodriguez, O.C.D., New York: Paulist Press, 1979. (Written by a sixteenth-century Spanish Carmelite, this book describes seven inward dwelling places into which the soul enters through the gateway of prayer, and in the seventh, which is in the centre, God dwells in the greatest splendour.)

Chapter 4

THE DISCIPLINE OF FASTING

The central ideal in fasting is the voluntary denial of an otherwise normal function for the sake of intense spiritual activity. There is nothing wrong with these normal functions in life; it is simply that there are times when we set them aside in order to concentrate. When we view fasting from this perspective we can see its reasonableness as well as its broader dimensions. The Bible deals with fasting in regard to food, but allow me to take the central principle and apply it to other aspects of contemporary culture.*

First, there is a need today to learn to fast from people. We have a tendency to just devour people, and we usually get severe heartburn from it! I suggest that we learn to fast from people not because we are antisocial but precisely because we love people intensely and when we are with them, we want to be able to do them good and not harm. The Discipline of solitude and the Discipline of community go hand in hand. Until we have learned to be alone we cannot be with people in a way that will help them, for we will bring to that relationship our own scatteredness. Conversely, until we have learned to be with people, being alone will be a dangerous thing, for it will cut us off from hurting, bleeding humanity.

*Some of the following ideas have appeared in a somewhat different form in another book of mine, *Freedom of Simplicity* (Triangle/S.P.C.K., 1981)

Second, let's learn times to fast from the media. It has always amazed me that many people seem incapable (or at least unwilling) to go through an entire day concentrating on a single thing. Their train of thought is constantly broken up by this demand and that – the newspaper, the radio, the television, the magazines. No wonder we feel fractured and fragmented. Obviously, there is a time for the media, but there is also a time to be without the media. We send our children to summer camp and they come back thrilled because "God spoke to me!" What happened at camp was simple: they merely got rid of enough distractions for a long enough period of time to concentrate. We can do that through the course of our ordinary days.

Third, I would suggest times of fasting from the telephone. The telephone is a wonderful invention, but it must not control us. I have known people who stop praying in order to answer the telephone! I want to let you in on a secret: you are under no obligation to answer that gadget every time it rings. In our home, when we are eating or when I am reading stories to the children, we do not answer the telephone because I want my boys to know they are more important than any phone call. And it is terribly offensive to interrupt an important conversation just to answer a machine.

Fourth, I would like to suggest the Discipline of fasting from billboards. I still remember the day I was driving on the Los Angeles freeway system when all of a sudden I realized that for one solid hour my mind had been dominated by the billboards. Now when I suggest that we fast from billboards, I do not mean that we should refrain from looking at them, but that the billboard should be a signal to us of another reality. When the ad man shouts out to us his four-letter obscenities, "More, more, more", let it remind us of another four-letter word, a rich, full-bodied word, "Less, less, less". When we are bombarded with bigger than life pictures of foxy ladies and well-fed babies, perhaps that can trigger in our minds another world, a world in which four hundred and sixty million people are the victims of acute hunger (ten thousand of them will be dead by this time tomorrow), a world in which a million hogs in Indiana have superior housing to a billion people on this planet.

That leads me to my fifth and final suggestion, which is that we discover times to fast from our gluttonous consumer culture that we find so comfortable. For our souls' sake, we need times when we go among Christ's favourites – the broken, the bruised, the dispossessed – not to preach to them but to learn from them. For the sake of our balance, for the sake of our sanity, we need times when we are among those who, in the words of Mahatma Gandhi, live an "eternal compulsory fast".

Fasting is a Spiritual Discipline ordained by God for the good of the Christian fellowship. May God find within us hearts that are open to appropriate this means of His grace.

Daily Scripture Readings

Sunday   – The example of Christ. Luke 4:1–13

Monday   – God's chosen fast. Isaiah 58:1–7

Tuesday   – A partial fast. Daniel 10:1–14

Wednesday – A normal fast. Nehemiah 1:4–11

Thursday   – An absolute fast. Esther 4:12–17

Friday   – The inauguration of the Gentile mission. Acts 13:1–3

Saturday   – The appointment of elders in the Churches. Acts 14:19–23

Study Questions

1. Check your first reaction to the thought of fasting?
   - _____ ugh
   - _____ hmmm
   - _____ wow!
   - _____ ok
   - _____ freedom
   - _____ you must be joking

2. How does Christian fasting differ from the hunger strike and health fasting?

3. Define "a normal fast", "a partial fast", and "an absolute fast".

4. What is the primary purpose of fasting?

5. How can fasting show what controls your life?

6. What is the most difficult thing about fasting for you?

7. Fast for two meals (twenty-four hours) and give the time saved to God. Record anything you learn from the experience.

8. Try fasting from the media for one week and see what you learn about yourself.

9. Discuss the question of whether fasting is only a cultural expression of Christian faith or whether it is for all cultures at all times.

10. In his day John Wesley required that every minister ordained in the Methodist Church regularly fast two days a week. Discuss the implications of such a requirement in our day.

Suggestions for Further Reading

Cartwright, Thomas, *The Holy Exercise of a True Fast*, London, 1610. (Written by a Puritan leader who was the first minister in

England, after the Reformation, to make clear the important distinction between fasting for health purposes and fasting for spiritual purposes.)

Ehret, Arnold, *Rational Fasting*, Beaumont: Ehret Literature Publishing Co., 1971. (A consideration of fasting from the perspective of physical health and well-being.)

Knox, John, *Order and Doctrine of a General Fast*, Edinburgh, 1565. (Written by the leader of the Scottish Reformation.)

Prince, Derek, *Shaping History Through Prayer & Fasting*, Old Tappan: Fleming H. Revell Company, 1973. (Filled with many interesting historical examples, this study by a leader in the charismatic movement seeks to show the impact of fasting upon societies.)

Rogers, Eric N., *Fasting: The Phenomenon of Self Denial*, Nashville: Thomas Nelson Inc., 1976. (A survey of fasting among the great religions of the world, including a study of fasting for political and health purposes.)

Smith, David R. *Fasting*. London: Rushworth Literature Enterprise Ltd, 1969. (An excellent study which includes in the back the best bibliography to be had on fasting.)

Smith, Fred W., *Journal Of A Fast*, New York: Ballantine Books, 1972. (The journal notations of a blue-collar worker who undertook an extended fast. It is filled with human interest and practical wisdom even though you may find some of his philosophical and theological comments strange to your ears.)

Wallis, Arthur, *God's Chosen Fast*, Eastbourne: Victory Press, 1969. (In my opinion the best single book on the market today in bringing together the theory and the practice of Christian fasting.)

Chapter 5

THE DISCIPLINE OF STUDY

The mind will always take on an order conforming to the order of whatever it concentrates upon. Once some friends gave us the loan of their beach house on the Oregon coast. It was a secluded spot where virtually the only building in sight was an old lighthouse on the far peninsula, and the only visitors were seagulls. The cabin had no TV and no telephone. There was a radio, but it didn't work. But there was a record player and two old records – the sound track from *Oklahoma* and *Johnny Appleseed*. How nice, I thought, one record for the children and one for the adults. In the course of a week I suppose we played those two records some fifty times. For months afterwards I found myself singing or humming those songs – in the shower, in board meetings, in church. I even sang them in my dreams. What happened was simple: unconsciously, the functioning of my mind began taking on the order of the music.

This is why the problem of mind pollution is so crucial. Now when I speak of mind pollution I am not thinking only of "bad" books, films and so on, but of mediocre books and films. You see, unless we set before ourselves a "habitual vision of greatness" we will surely degenerate. This is why it is ruinous to have so much of our Christian literature of such poor literary quality. The sad fact of the modern world is that, in the main, men do not read at all, and many women are captives to the escapist romance novel which is of such poor quality that it should not even be considered literature. We simply must raise our sights.

Have you ever pondered why people do not read in our day? It is certainly not because we lack the time. In 1981 America spent 75,000 man-years playing video games* and God knows how many more thousands (or millions?) entranced by television. Though I have yet to join the video-game craze (I'm too self-conscious), I certainly don't mind a TV programme now and then, but abject slavery is another thing altogether. This week my son's fifth-grade teacher polled the class on their weekend activities and found the majority of the class watched over fifteen hours of TV and read under one hour. Only one other student besides Joel had watched under two hours of TV and had read around seven hours.

In order to raise our sights and take the Spiritual Discipline of study seriously may I put in a plug for disciplined reading. In my courses at the university I usually require seven or eight books in each class. At first students think they are being sent to the guillotine, but by the end of the term, they are thrilled to discover such a rich world, a world that makes *pac man* or *The Dukes of Hazard* look drab and dull.

Our children are required to read each evening. Both boys go to their room at 8:00 p.m. (Notice, this means that we must say "No" to most evening church meetings and entertainment extravaganzas, though we will make rare exceptions.) Joel, our ten-year-old, is allowed to read for one hour. Nathan, our seven-year-old, reads for fifteen minutes. And with only minimal encouragement from us, they have taken to some substantial literature – Joel is presently devouring *The Lord of the Rings*. We also read together out loud. Recently Nathan has requested *The Chronicles of Narnia* and so (although Joel has read it many times) we all sit together after supper and share in the wonderful adventures

Time magazine, 18 January 1982.

of Peter, Susan, Edmund and Lucy in the magical land of Narnia. Next we plan to read aloud *The Pilgrim's Progress*.

Study is of course a much larger Discipline than reading, and many who read never study, but reading is an important element in study and should not be lost. I'm sure you will find God waiting for you as you engage in the ministry of study.

Daily Scripture Readings

Sunday — The call to study. Proverbs 1:1–9, 23:12, 23

Monday — The source of truth. James 1:5, Hebrews 4:11–13, II Timothy 3:16–17

Tuesday — What to study. Philippians 4:8–9, Colossians 3:1–17

Wednesday — The value of Study. Luke 10:38–42

Thursday — Active study. Ezra 7:10, James 1:19–25

Friday · — Study in the evangelistic enterprise. Acts 17:1–3 & 10–12, 19:8–10

Saturday — The study of a non-verbal book. Proverbs 24:30–34

Study Questions

1. Why does study more fully bring about the purpose of the Spiritual Disciplines, which is the transformation of the individual? (I.e. what does it do that other Disciplines do not do?)

2. What is study? (This is an important question because there is a general ignorance among Christians regarding its answer.)

3. Have you ever had any experience with the study of non-verbal books?

4. The four steps into study which I give are repetition, concentration, comprehension and reflection. Which of these four do you feel is the most important in bringing about the goal of the transformation of the individual?

5. Outside of the Bible, which book has had the most profound impact upon your own life? Why?

6. On page 60 I write, "In study we are not seeking spiritual ecstasy; in fact, ecstasy can be a hindrance." How could it be a hindrance?

7. List three things which you could do this next week in order to follow the dictum of Socrates, "Know thyself".

8. Study a plant or tree for ten minutes and write down what you learn from the experience.

9. Why does study produce joy?

10. Consider the purchase of a serious book on the Spiritual life to read this next week.

Suggestions for Further Reading

Adler, Mortimer J., *How To Read A Book*, New York: Simon and Schuster, 1958. (The standard by which all of us measure our efforts. Essential reading for all who want to read correctly.)

Blamires, Harry, *The Christian Mind*, London: S.P.C.K., 1963. (A careful analysis of the assumptions of the contemporary culture and a call to a more authentic Christian world view by a former student of C.S. Lewis.)

Rutherford, Jean, and others, *How To Study The Bible*, ed. John B. Job, Downers Grove: InterVarsity Press, 1972. (Presents some eight approaches to Bible study such as character study, word study, theme study, etc.)

Sire, James E., *How To Read Slowly: A Christian Guide to Reading With the Mind*, Downers Grove: InterVarsity Press, 1979. (Helps Christians read so that the world view of the author becomes obvious.)

Stott, John R.W., *Understanding The Bible*, London: Scripture Union, 1972. (An exceedingly helpful resource for personal Bible study covering issues of interpretation and authority as well as the basic flow of the Biblical story.)

Trueblood, Elton, *The New Man For Our Time*, San Francisco: Harper & Row, Publishers, Inc., 1970. (A plea for Christians to love God with the mind as well as the heart and the hands.)

Chapter 6

THE DISCIPLINE OF SIMPLICITY

Simplicity is openness, unself-consciousness, naturalness. It is the opposite of subtlety, cunning, duplicity.

Where simplicity abounds words can be taken at face value: there is no hidden agenda. And yet, simplicity is not synonymous with "easy to understand". Jesus was not easy to understand, nor was Paul, but both were characterized by simplicity of speech. Their intent was not to confuse or deceive but to clarify and illuminate.

Simplicity frees us from the tyranny of the self, the tyranny of things and the tyranny of people.*

The self clamours for attention, self-recognition, applause. Through artful deception it appears to be younger, wiser, richer, saintlier than is actually the case. It will go to extravagant lengths to seem to belong to the intelligentsia. In meetings it will quote authors it has never read or maintain a discreet silence in supposed superiority over so uneducated a group.

Confront and challenge the tyranny of the self with the following questions:

Am I pretending to be an expert where I am only an amateur?
Do I really read the books I quote?

*These brief words are adopted from material in Albert Day's book *Discipline and Discovery*.

Do I use rhetoric as a curtain to conceal my true intentions?

Do I give the impression of being more godly (or more profane, whichever will give more status in the group) than I truly am?

Do I try to impress people with my degrees, titles, or honours?

Simplicity also prevails against the tyranny of things. Out of fear that others might discover who we are, we create an artificial world of ostentatious display, extravagant ornamentation and pretentious style. We call upon the beautician, the tailor and the dressmaker to create an impression of perpetual youth. We buy clothes, cars and houses beyond our means in a frantic attempt to appear successful.

Rebuke the tyranny of things with the following questions:

Am I living contentedly within my income?

Do I act my age?

Am I a compulsive buyer?

Do I try to impress people with gadgets?

Do I buy what I can afford and what my responsibility to the poor suggests?

Finally, there is the tyranny of people. What horrendous gymnastics we will put ourselves through just to ensure that others will have a good opinion of us! How desperately and sincerely we labour to create the right impression. Instead of becoming good we resort to all sorts of devices to make people think we are good.

Joyfully attack the tyranny of people with the following questions:

Can I allow an unfavourable comment about myself to stand, without any need to straighten out the matter?

In recounting events do I shift the story ever so slightly to make myself appear in a more favourable light?

Must I always make excuses for my behaviour?

Do I aim at excellence in my work without regard for what people may say or think?
Can I accept compliments freely without any need to shrug them off in self-conscious modesty?

Only the simple are free. All others are tyrannized by the ambitious self, the demand for recognition through things, and a preoccupation with the opinions of others. François Fénelon declared, "Simplicity is an uprightness of soul which prevents self-consciousness. Verily such simplicity is a great treasure!"

Daily Scripture Readings

Sunday   – Simplicity as singleness of heart. Matthew 6:19–24

Monday   – Simplicity as trust. Matthew 6:25–34

Tuesday   – Simplicity as obedience. Genesis 15

Wednesday – The generosity of simplicity. Leviticus 25:8–12

Thursday   – Simplicity in speech. Matthew 5:33–37, James 5:12

Friday   – Simplicity and justice. Amos 5:11–15, 24, Luke 4:16–21

Saturday   – The freedom from covetousness. Luke 12:13–34

Study Questions

1. What are the two aspects of simplicity and why are *both* essential?

2. In one paragraph, attempt to set forth the biblical teaching on possessions.

3. What would the concept of the year of Jubilee look like in modern society (Lev. 25:8–12)?

4. What do I set forth as the focal point for an understanding of Christian simplicity?

5. What are the three inward attitudes of simplicity? Of the three, which do you find the most difficult for you personally?

6. What is the great danger in setting forth an outward expression to Christian simplicity? Why *must* we take the risk?

7. Which of the ten controlling principles for outward simplicity is the most helpful to you? Are there any you feel are unrealistic?

8. What is producing an addiction in you?

9. Wrestle with the implications of the ninth principle. (Reject anything that will breed the oppression of others.)

10. List one thing which you could do this next week to simplify your life. Do it.

Suggestions for Further Reading

Cooper, John C., *Finding A Simpler Life*, Philadelphia: United Church Press, 1974. (Lays the groundwork for an authentic vision of simplicity in modern society.)

Cooper, John C., *The Joy of the Plain Life*, Nashville: Impact Books, 1981. (A joyous celebration of the gift of simplicity. Cooper has made his book particularly helpful by having individuals from many walks of life share at the end of each chapter their practical experiences of the chapter theme.)

Edwards, Tilden, *Living Simply Through the Day*, New York: Paulist Press, 1977. (Beginning with a personal pilgrimage, Tilden Edwards helps to free us from our anxiety-ridden culture by simple exercises which are tied to our daily experiences of eating, playing, serving, sleeping, etc.)

Eller, Vernard, *The Simple Life*, Grand Rapids: Eerdmans Publishing Co., 1973. (A look at inward simplicity through the eyes of the gospel records and the writings of Søren Kierkegaard.)

Foster, Richard, *Freedom of Simplicity*, London: Triangle/S.P.C.K., 1981. (Attempts to place simplicity within the context of the whole of Christian devotion and to bring together the various emphases upon inner and outer simplicity.)

Gish, Arthur G., *Beyond the Rat Race*, New Canaan: Keats Publishing Inc., 1973. (Art Gish launches an uncompromising attack on materialism and a vigorous call to outward simplicity.)

Hengel, Martin, *Property and Riches in the Early Church*, Philadelphia: Fortress Press, 1974. (A scholarly study of the Christian approach to property and riches from the time of Christ – there is also a brief discussion of Old Testament views – up to about the fourth century. Extensive attention is given to the Ante-Nicene Fathers.)

Longacre, Doris Janzen, *Living More With Less*, London: Hodder & Stoughton Ltd., 1982. (A follow-up to her bestselling *More-With-Less Cookbook*. This volume is filled with a wealth of practical suggestions by Mennonites throughout the world.)

Sider, Ronald J., *Rich Christians In An Age of Hunger: A Biblical Study*, London: Hodder & Stoughton Ltd., 1978. (Extremely valuable biblical and practical study of the question of justice in modern society. Must reading.)

Taylor, Richard K., *Economics and the Gospel*, Philadelphia: United Church Press, 1973. (A powerful analysis of economic justice in the context of Christian ethics.)

Ziegler, Edward K., *Simple Living*, Elgin: The Brethren Press, 1974. (A look at simplicity from the perspective of the Church of the Brethren.)

Chapter 7

THE DISCIPLINE OF SOLITUDE

Henri Nouwen has noted that, "Without solitude it is virtually impossible to live a spiritual life." Why is this so? Because in solitude we are freed *from* our bondage to people and our inner compulsions, and we are freed *to* love God and know compassion for others.

To enter solitude we must disregard what others think of us. Who will understand this call to aloneness? Even our closest friends will see it as a terrible waste of precious time and as rather selfish and self-centred. But, oh, what liberty is released in our hearts when we let go of the opinions of others! The less we are mesmerized by human voices, the more we are able to hear the divine Voice. The less we are bound by others' expectations, the more we are open to God's expectations.

But in solitude we die not only to others but also to ourselves. To be sure, at first we thought solitude was a way to recharge our batteries in order to enter life's many competitions with new vigour and strength. In time, however, we found that solitude did not give us power to win the rat race; on the contrary, it taught us to ignore it altogether. Slowly, we found ourselves letting go of our inner compulsions to win and our frantic efforts to attain. In the stillness our false, busy selves were unmasked and seen for the impostors they truly were.

It is out of our liberation from others and self that our ears become open to hear and our eyes unveiled to see the goodness of God. We can love God because we do not have to love the world. Through our solitude an open inner space has been created through which God finds us. In solitude we experience a second (and third, and fourth, and fifth . . .) conversion. In a deeper more profound way we turn from the idols of the marketplace to the glory of God in the face of Jesus Christ. God takes this useless discipline, this wasted time, to make us His friend.

A happy by-product of becoming the friend of God is an increased compassion for others. Once we have peered into the abyss of our own vanity we can never again look at the struggles of others with condescending superiority. Once we have faced the demons of despair in our own aloneness, we can never again pass off lightly the quiet depression and sad loneliness of those we meet. We become one with all who hurt and are afraid. We are free to give them the greatest gift we possess – the gift of ourselves.

The private retreat is one way to nurture solitude. In *Celebration* I shared several ideas regarding what to do in a private retreat; however, it is of utmost importance that we do not lose sight of our major work on retreat. It can be said in one word – PRAYER. We enter the terrifying silences to listen to God, to experience communion. This purpose needs to be kept before us because, at first, time thus spent will seem so useless, so wasted. We will soon be severely tempted to make "good use of our time" by reading many books or writing many pages. What we must clearly understand and underscore is that our real task on retreat is to create a space in our lives where God can reach us. Once that space has been created we wait quietly, expectantly, for the work from this point on belongs to God. And I have found Him most eager to usher us into the Holy of Holies and share with us the glories of the Kingdom of God.

In *Fruits of Solitude* William Penn observed that solitude is "A school few care to learn in, tho' none instructs us better". May we be among the few that care to learn through this merciful means of God's grace.

Daily Scripture Readings

Sunday — The freedom to control the tongue. James 3:1–12, Luke 23:6–9

Monday — Prayer and solitude. Matthew 6:5–6, Luke 5:16

Tuesday — The insights of solitude. Psalm 8

Wednesday — The dark night of the soul. Jeremiah 20:7–18

Thursday — The solitude of the garden. Matthew 26:36–46

Friday — The solitude of the cross. Matthew 27:32–50

Saturday — The compassion that comes from solitude. Matthew 9:35–38, 23:37

Study Questions

1. What is the difference between loneliness and solitude? Which do you experience more?

2. Why do we need both solitude and community in order to function with spiritual success?

3. Why do you think that solitude and silence are so closely connected?

4. What is the "sacrifice of fools"? Have you ever been guilty?

5. Have you ever had any experience akin to Catherine de Haeck Doherty's, "All in me is silent and . . . I am immersed in the silence of God"? If so you might want to share it with someone, if not you might want to ponder the reason for the lack.

6. Have you ever experienced a "dark night of the soul"?

7. I mention five possible steps into solitude. Which one would you find most helpful at this point in your life?

8. What keeps you from solitude?

9. What practical reordering of your life could be done in order to create more space for God?

10. What experience in solitude would you like to have, two years from now, that you do not presently possess? Would you be willing this week to plan it into your schedule for sometime in the next twenty-four months?

Suggestions for Further Reading

Doherty, Catherine de Hueck, *Poustinia: Christian Spirituality of the East for Western Man*, London: Collins (William) Sons & Co. Ltd., 1977. (A sensitive and highly applicable discussion of how Western culture can find space for the life of solitude.)

Helen Waddell, trans., *The Desert Fathers*, London: Constable & Co. Ltd. (Contains many of the wise sayings of the Desert Fathers as well as the stories of their experiences.)

Hoyland, Geoffrey, *The Use of Silence*, Inner Life Series, number five, London: S.P.C.K., 1955. (A pamphlet on the Quaker experience of the "Living Silence" on both individual and corporate levels.)

Maloney, George A., S.J., *Alone With The Alone*, Notre Dame: Ave Maria Press, 1982. (Helps the individual enter into the experience of God – the Alone – through the format of an eight-day retreat.)

Nee, Watchman, *Deep Calleth Unto Deep*, Los Angeles: The Stream. (A tiny booklet which beckons you to the inner sanctuary of the soul.)

Nouwen, Henri J.M., *Out of Solitude*, Notre Dame: Ave Maria Press, 1974. (Three brief messages on the fruit of solitude in contemporary ministry.)

Nouwen, Henri J.M., *The Genesee Diary*, New York: Doubleday, 1976. (Going from an active life of teaching at Yale Divinity School to a seven-month experience in a Trappist Monastery, Nouwen shares the insights of his sojourn.)

Nouwen, Henri J.M., *The Way of the Heart*, London: Darton, Longman & Todd Ltd., 1981. (A meaningful interpretation into the twentieth century of the wisdom of the Desert Fathers.)

Oats, Wayne, *Nurturing Silence in a Noisy Heart*, New York: Doubleday, 1979. (Most helpful counsel on how inner solitude can take up residence in the midst of our busy lives.)

Chapter 8

THE DISCIPLINE OF SUBMISSION

In submission we recognize the legitimate authority of others over us. It is nothing more than the simple understanding that "no man is an island". Life in community is our rightful home: relationships with other human beings are our inheritance. To confess our commitment to community means to confess our commitment to mutual subordination. Peter crystallized this principle in the simple phrase "honour all men" (I Peter 2:17), and Paul set forth the idea in what must be considered the most memorable sentence on the subject, "Be subject to one another out of reverence for Christ" (Eph. 5:21).

Submission is a concept as broad as life itself and a Discipline found throughout Scripture. It raises issues that are deep and difficult: issues of submission to the ways of God, issues of submission to the state, issues of submission to the Christian fellowship, issues of submission in the Christian household and much more. As we hammer out our understanding of these matters we will always want to hold before us the life and death of Christ as the divine paradigm by which all the verbs of Christian submission are to be conjugated.

In regard to the Christian family the New Testament dared to flesh out the meaning of submission in a body of instructions which Martin Luther called the *Haustafeln*, or

"The Table of Instructions for the Christian Household".*
This teaching was a gracious way of setting forth the function
of submission within the family in first-century culture. In
our day, however, this body of instructions has been terribly
garbled and abused. The following distortions of submission
reveal in part the knack we moderns have for taking the best
teaching and using it for the worst ends.

The Doormat – This is the person who allows others to
misuse and abuse him to such an extent that he is treated as a
thing rather than a person. In a false and unhealthy submission he allows others to walk over him as one would a
doormat. His opinion is neither sought nor desired, and in
time he loses the ability even to have an opinion. Such a
person soon becomes an object rather than a subject – a
housekeeper rather than a wife, a bread-winner rather than a
husband. He is defined by what he can produce rather than
by who he is. In the end he has been "thing-a-fied".

The Pleaser – This is the person who wants more than
anything else to avoid conflict. He sees a fight coming a mile
away and will go to any lengths to keep it from occurring. It is
comical (and tragic) to find two "pleasers" married to each
other.

"What would you like to do tonight, Honey?"

"Whatever you would like, Dear."

"Well, I just want to make you happy."

"And that is exactly what I want to do for you. I'll do
anything that will make you happy."

"If it would please you, I would be glad to go out to
dinner."

"I'd love to if it would make you happy."

"Fine, what kind of food do you like?"

"Whatever you would enjoy, Dear!"

. . . and on it goes *ad nauseam*.

The Dependant – This is the person who fears making
decisions like the plague. Rather than own up to the

---

*Eph. 5:21 ff., Col. 3:18 ff., Titus 2:4 ff., and I Pet. 2:1 ff.

maturing process of choice, he finds refuge in a pseudo-submission which allows others to make all his decisions. Fear is at the root of such submission – fear of leading others in the wrong way, fear of making an ill-timed decision, fear of blame if programmes fail. And so he never causes waves, he never offends, and he never accomplishes anything of lasting value.

The Manipulator – This is the person who follows all of the outward rules of submission, but employs every subtle trick to get his own way. Acts of mercy are done to put us into his debt. Words of kindness are given to win us to his side. While fully agreeing with our decision, little hints of doubt are sown through a look or a gesture or perhaps a slight quavering of the voice. Often the practice is so ingrained that the individual himself does not realize that he has taken control of every situation.

The distortions that I have shared are, for the most part, religiously approved means to dehumanizing and destructive ends. But Jesus Christ calls us to a more excellent way – a way of love and compassion, a way of submission and service.

Daily Scripture Readings

Sunday   – The call to submission. Mark 8:34, John 12:24–26

Monday   – The example of Christ. Philippians 2:1–11

Tuesday   – The example of Abraham. Genesis 22:1–19

Wednesday – The example of Paul. Galatians 2:19–21

Thursday   – Submission in the marketplace. Matthew 5:38–48

Friday   – Submission in the family. Ephesians 5:21–6:9, I Peter 3:1–9

Saturday   – Submission with reference to the State. Romans 13:1–10, Acts 4:13–20, 5:27–29, 16:35–39

Study Questions

1. How have you seen the Discipline of submission abused?

2. What is the freedom in submission? Have you entered into any experience of this?

3   I write, "In submission we are at last free to value other people." What is it about submission that allows this to happen?

4. Why did I begin the chapter by discussing what submission does before I define what it is?

5. What images come to your mind when you think of the word "self-denial"?

6. Why was Jesus' teaching on submission so revolutionary?

7. In one brief paragraph attempt to summarize what you feel is the teaching of the epistles on submission.

8. What are the limits of submission and why is that important?

9. Of the seven acts of submission, which one do you feel you need to work on most?

10. What do you think it would mean to be in submission to the ways of God? (Ponder this question carefully because it does not yield to pat answers.)

Suggestions for Further Reading

The lack of books below does not reflect my unawareness of contemporary writings but my unwillingness to commend them. The idea of submission pervaded the world view of the old writers (think of à Kempis' *Imitation* or Fénelon's *Christian Perfection*) but it is a strange mutation to modern writers. For the most part contemporary discussions are limited to two small corners of the Discipline – the man/woman question and the Shepherding or Discipling concept in certain charismatic circles. To my knowledge, no one has provided us with a full-blown intelligent discussion of this subject.

Butt, Howard, *The Velvet Covered Brick*, New York: Harper & Row, Publishers, 1973. (The experience of one man's attempt to take the biblical concepts of "authority" and "submission" and hammer them out on the hard anvil of the business world.)

Smedes, Lewis B., *Love Within Limits*, Tring: Lion Publishing, 1979. (Based upon I Corinthians 13, Lewis Smedes defines love as "the power that moves us to respond to a neighbour's need with no expectation of reward" and in so doing defines the fundamental principle out of which the Discipline of submission operates.)

Yoder, John Howard, *The Politics of Jesus*, Grand Rapids: Eerdmans Publishing Company, 1972. (Impressive in its scholarship and its insight. Contains two important chapters on the subject; "Revolutionary Subordination" and "Let Every Soul Be Subject: Romans 13 and the Authority of the State". He has given us an excellent foundation for a modern understanding of the Discipline of submission for our day; we now need someone who could build upon it.)

Chapter 9

THE DISCIPLINE OF SERVICE

In his most famous teaching on service Jesus concluded, "For the Son of man also came not to be served but to serve, and to give his life as a ransom for many" (Mark 10:45). Our Lord's unique service of redemption through the Cross is unrepeatable. However, we are called to serve through the many little deaths of going beyond self. And as we live out our lives for the good of others, amazingly we find ourselves, we discover our sense of place.

When Paul spoke of the generosity of the believers in Macedonia he noted that "first they gave themselves" (II Cor. 8:5). This is the first mark of the Discipline of service. Service cannot be done *in absentia*. It necessitates our personal involvement. Like St Francis of Assisi we must touch the leper, we must reach out to the one in need.

How counter this is to the modern call to watch out for number one. (And may I just add that if you are driven by the need to watch out for number one, God help you, because no one else will!) But in the Kingdom of God we can let go of such drives because we are able to cast all our care upon Him, for He cares for us (I Peter 5:7).

One reality must be clearly understood in the life of service. The very fact that we are finite means that to say "Yes" to one task of necessity means saying "No" to other tasks. When I said "Yes" to the service of writing this study guide, I had to say "No" to many good and noble tasks. I could not go to special meetings, serve on worthy committees, speak at important gatherings, or even counsel with needy people. To give in to these other quite important ministries would mean failing to serve through writing.

Listen to this heartbreaking story of a young mother who in the beginning thought service meant saying "Yes" to any and all demands upon her time and energy. "Someone was *always* dropping in for a visit and staying late, often till two a.m. until we were exhausted. We had *no* time to be together as a family. The routine and discipline of our two small children were disturbed to the point that they were being raised by other people while we had Bible studies and shared with needy folk. The relationship between my husband and me suffered because we were exhausted and had very little time alone. I became the dumping place for preschoolers until I was just about berserk from the responsibility. I became the maker of clothes for many of the women who were working outside the home and simply didn't have time to sew. I became 'the listener' who spent so much time on the phone that there were *many* days that my children's lunches were fixed from things I could reach from the phone and my housework was untouched due to serving others. And on and on it went until I finally cracked, put my foot down and learned to say 'No'." This deeply committed woman was having to say "No" to her children and husband by saying "Yes" to the demands of other folk.

The point is that we are not omnipresent and we should admit as much. The Discipline of service asks us to serve irrespective of class or status distinctions, but it also recognizes our human limitations. Love is a reasoned concern for the wellbeing of all. If I bring people into my home under the supposition that I am serving them, but in the process I destroy my wife and children, I am not living in love. Most likely I am merely gratifying my egocentric need to feel righteous rather than entering into true service. Admittedly the balance is not easy to maintain – significant matters in life seldom are. That is the reason for discipline:

remember, the disciplined person is the person who can do what needs to be done when it needs to be done.

Discernment and obedience are the keys. Learning when to say "No" is important: so is learning when to say "Yes". Once we have been burned by a compulsive "Yes" the temptation will be to say "No" to everything, or at least those things we find distasteful. But that can be as enslaving as the former state. What we need is to learn the rhythm of the Holy Spirit so that our "Yes" or "No" to calls of service will arise out of that harmony.

Daily Scripture Readings

Sunday   — The call to service. Matthew 20:20–28

Monday   — The sign of service. John 13:1–17

Tuesday   — The commitment of service. Exodus 21:2, 5–6, I Corinthians 9:19

Wednesday — The attitude of service. Colossians 3:23–25

Thursday   — Service in the Christian fellowship. Romans 12:9–13

Friday   — The ministry of small things. Matthew 25:31–39

Saturday   — Service exemplified. Luke 10:29–37

Study Questions

1. If the towel is the sign of service, how can that sign be manifested in twentieth-century culture?

2. Did you find the discussion of self-righteous service as contrasted with true service:

   _____ right on
   _____ terribly idealistic
   _____ naïve
   _____ faithful to Scripture but impractical for today
   _____ strange?

   Discuss your answer with others.

3. Debate the notion that love is a "reasoned concern for the wellbeing of all", and consider its implications with reference to service.

4. In the book I mention that service works humility into our lives. What in the world do you think humility means? (i.e. what does humility look like?)

5. Have you ever allowed yourself to be taken advantage of and had it turn out to be destructive rather than redemptive?

6. Does the believer have rights that should not be given up for the sake of others?

7. What would the service of hiddenness look like in your life?

8. This next week see if you can find one way each day to exercise the service of common courtesy.

9. When should you say "No" to the demands people place upon your time and attention?

10. Give this prayer a try some time this month: "Lord Jesus, I would so appreciate it if you would bring me someone today whom I can serve."

Suggestions for Further Reading

Bonhoeffer, Dietrich, *Life Together*, trans. John W. Doberstein, London: SCM Press Ltd., 1954. (Powerful insights into the life of service, solitude, and confession. Essential reading.)

Greenleaf, Robert K., *The Servant As Leader*, Cambridge: Centre for Applied Studies, 1973. (A thirty-seven page essay which is intended as the first of four pamphlets on service as it relates to individuals, trustees and institutions.)

Greenleaf, Robert K., *Servant Leadership*, New York: Paulist Press, 1977. (A seminal work on the nature of legitimate power and greatness by one who clearly understands both the world of corporate management and the Christian witness to service.)

Mains, Karen Burton, *Open Heart Open Home*, Elgin: David C. Cook Publishing Co., 1981. (An encouraging call to the ministry of Christian hospitality.)

Swindoll, Charles R., *Improving Your Serve*, London: Hodder & Stoughton Ltd., 1983. (Helpful sermons on the art of unselfish living.)

Chapter 10

THE DISCIPLINE OF CONFESSION

Confession is a corporate Discipline because sin both offends God and creates a wound in the Christian fellowship. In the early centuries of the Christian era forgiveness and reconciliation involved a lengthy process of healing by which the offender was restored to health through the ministry of the total Christian community. In the early Middle Ages it was turned increasingly into a private sacrament, and following the Reformation Protestants began to view it more and more as a matter exclusively between the individual and God. But in the beginning, confession was not the privatistic event it is today; in fact, in Matthew 18 Jesus expressed its essential communal nature and explained how forgiveness can come into the community without destroying it. It is God who does the forgiving, but often He chooses human beings as the channel of His forgiving grace.

Human beings are such that "life together" always involves them in hurting one another in some way. And forgiveness is essential in a community of hurt and hurtful persons. In experiencing forgiveness it is important to understand what it is *not*. Four things are often mistaken for forgiveness.

First, some imagine forgiveness means a pretending that it doesn't really matter. "Oh, that's all right, it really didn't hurt me anyway!" we say. That is not forgiveness; it is lying. And love and lies do not mix well. The truth is that these things matter a great deal, and it does not help to avoid the issue. What we need is not avoidance but reconciliation.

Second, some think that forgiveness means a ceasing to hurt. There is the belief that if we continue to hurt, we must have failed to truly forgive. That is simply not true. Hurting is not evil. We may hurt for a very long time to come. Forgiveness does not mean that we will stop hurting.

Third, many would have us believe that forgiveness means forgetting. "Forgive and forget," as we often say. But the truth of the matter is that we cannot forget. We remember; the difference will be that we no longer need or desire to use the memory against others. The memory remains, the vindictiveness leaves. The attempt to force people to forget what cannot be forgotten only puts them in bondage and confuses the meaning of forgiveness.

Fourth, many assume that to forgive means to pretend that the relationship is just the same as before the offence. But this is simply not the case. The relationship will never be the same again. We might just as well make peace with that *fact*. By the grace of God it may be a hundred times better, but it will never be the same.

True confession and forgiveness brings joy to the Christian community and healing to the parties involved. Most wonderful of all it spells reconciliation with God the Father, for as the beloved apostle said so long ago, "If we confess our sins, he is faithful and just, and will forgive our sins and cleanse us from all unrighteousness" (I John 1:9).

Daily Scripture Readings

Sunday   – The need for confession and forgiveness. Isaiah 59:1–9, Romans 3:10–18

Monday   – The promise of forgiveness. Jeremiah 31:34, Matthew 26:28, Ephesians 1:7

Tuesday   – The assurance of forgiveness. I John 1:5–10

Wednesday – Jesus Christ our adequate Saviour, Mediator and Advocate. II Corinthians 6:21, I Timothy 2:5, I John 2:1

Thursday   – A parable of confession. Luke 15:11–24

Friday   – Authority and forgiveness. Matthew 16:19, 18:18, John 20:23

Saturday   – The ministry of the Christian fellowship. James 5:13–16

Study Questions

1. In your own words try to describe the theology which lies behind the Discipline of confession.

2. What are the three advantages to formalized confession? Are there disadvantages?

3. I mention three things that are necessary for a good confession. Which of the three do you find most difficult to experience?

4. What does the idea of living "under the cross" mean in reference to confession?

5. List two or three dangers that you could imagine would accompany the exercise of the Christian Discipline of confession?

6. Does absolution indicate the forgiveness of sins or does it effect it?

7. When is the Discipline of confession an unhealthy preoccupation with sin and when is it a proper recognition of our need for forgiveness?

8. How would you distinguish between false guilt and genuine guilt?

9. St Augustine calls the sacraments of baptism and communion the *verba visibilia* (visible words) of our forgiveness, and John Stott notes that "Baptism, being unique and unrepeatable, is the sacrament of our once-for-all justification: Holy Communion, being repeatedly enjoyed, is the sacrament of our daily forgiveness. By them we are assured, audibly and visibly, of our acceptance and forgiveness." What is your reaction to this idea?

10. Some time this week spend fifteen minutes in silence before God, inviting Him to reveal anything within that needs to be confessed.

Suggestions for Further Reading

Augsburger, David, *Caring Enough To Forgive*, Ventura: Regal Books, 1981. (A forceful and perceptive discussion not only of the value of true forgiveness but also of the destructiveness of false forgiveness.)

Betz, Otto, ed., *Making Sense of Confession*, Franciscan Herald Press, 1969. (From a Roman Catholic perspective it contains helpful suggestions on how children and teenagers are nurtured in the Discipline of confession.)

Cornwall, Judson, *Let Us Enjoy Forgiveness*, Old Tappan: Fleming H. Revell Company, 1978. (A very readable study of divine forgiveness and exactly how that sets us free to love God and enjoy him for ever.)

Haring, Bernard, *Shalom: Peace. The Sacrament of Reconciliation.* Slough: St Paul Publications, 1980. (A vigorous description of the sacrament of penance from a Roman Catholic perspective.)

Scanlan, Michael, T.O.R., *The Power in Penance: Confession and the Holy Spirit*, Notre Dame: Ave Maria Press, 1972. (A powerful little booklet which brings fresh vitality to an ancient practice in the Catholic Church as a result of the charismatic renewal.)

Schlink, M. Basilea, *Repentance: The Joy-Filled Life*, London: Lakeland Paperbacks, 1969. (A slender but helpful work by the leader of the Mary Sisterhood, a Lutheran order in Germany.)

Stott, John R.W., *Confess Your Sins*, Waco: Word Books, 1974. (An extremely helpful discussion of the forms of confession as well as the meaning of reconciliation by the leading evangelical Anglican of our day.)

Chapter 11

THE DISCIPLINE OF WORSHIP

On one occasion we are told that St Francis of Assisi "Rejoiced greatly in Spirit, and he raised his face toward Heaven and stood for a long time with his mind absorbed in God." He entered worship.

Caught up into God, Juliana of Norwich exclaimed, "I saw Him, and sought Him: and I had Him, I wanted Him . . . he will be seeing and He will be sought: He will be abided and He will be trusted." She entered worship.

Worship is something that happens. It is experience. When we speak of having a "worship service" we are usually referring to the various elements of worship – hymns, Scripture readings, preaching, Holy Communion, liturgy. All of these may *lead* us to worship – but worship is much more than any of these expressions. The expressions are important because they are the means of God's grace, but it is quite possible to do them all without worship.

Worship centres in the experience of reality. Whatever ushers us into the Divine Presence should be welcomed. Whatever hinders a genuine encounter with the living Christ should be shunned! The Biblical requirements for worship include such matters as confession, adoration, proclamation and so on, but the Bible does not hold us to any universal wineskin or form in which worship must be contained. What we are to be committed to is reality – real worship, real confession, real praise, real adoration. If particular forms at particular times bring us more fully into worship, we are free to use them; if not, too bad for the forms. We are free to use the highest liturgy, no form at all, or anything in between so long as it brings us into real worship. The forms of worship must always be subject to the reality of worship.

Christ alone is the leader of worship, and it is He who decides what is needed and when it is needed. We should recognize and welcome the free exercise of all the Spiritual gifts, as they are used and directed by the Spirit. Christ puts His Word in the mouth of whomever he chooses, and He confirms this same Word in the hearts of the members of His community. If there is any excess He will raise up a prophet to bring the needed correction.

All these lofty words about the priority of reality over forms might make you think that I have little use for worship forms. Nothing could be further from the truth. Worship forms are absolutely essential if we are to enflesh the reality of worship. As long as we are finite we must have forms. And so we bring our bodies, minds, and spirits before God to give Him the glory due His name. We offer the sacrifice of our lips – our singing, our praising, our preaching, our confessing. We offer Him the sacrifice of our bodies – our listening hearts, our Eucharistic celebration, our obedient lives. And it is important to do these things whether we feel like doing them or not. Often I come into a worship experience and must honestly confess, "Lord, I do not feel like worshipping, I do not feel righteous, I'm tired and distracted in both body and spirit, but I want to give You this time. This hour belongs to You. I love You and to the best of my ability want to give You the glory due Your name. Therefore, I will sing and pray and listen and ask that in Your mercy You will free my spirit to worship You." And as I do this, often something seems to let go inside: perhaps it is the release of an old fear, or a little bitterness or maybe just a tightfisted determination to come into God. When this happens then the singing of hymns, the reading of Scripture, the confession of sin, the preaching of the Word, the receiving of Communion lead me into praise and adoration, which in turn opens the inner sanctuary of the soul into worship.

In this context may I lift up one form of worship which has a very ancient tradition but has fallen on hard times in our century. It is the use of the dance. For a thousand years Christians did a simple dance movement called the tripudium to many of their hymns. It worked well with any song in 2/2, 3/4, or 4/4 time. As they sang worshippers would take three steps forward, one step back, three steps forward, one step back. In doing this Christians were actually proclaiming a theology with their feet. They were declaring Christ's victory in an evil world, a victory that moves the Church forward but not without setbacks. This simple way to worship with the body can be used in any number of informal worship settings. It can even be done in the sanctuary provided the aisles are wide enough to accommodate three or four abreast, and then worshippers can march around the sanctuary singing the great hymns of the faith.

Above all worship leads us to Christ the Centre, as Bernard of Clairvaux put it so well:

> Jesus, Thou Joy of loving hearts!
> Thou Fount of life! Thou Light of men!
> From the best bliss that earth imparts,
> We turn unfilled to Thee again.

Daily Scripture Readings

Sunday   — Worship in spirit and truth. John 4:19–24

Monday   — Communion: the essence of worship. John 6:52–58, 63

Tuesday   — The life of worship. Ephesians 5:18–20, Colossians 3:16–17

Wednesday – The Lord high and lifted up. Isaiah 6:1–8

Thursday – Sing to the Lord. Psalm 96

Friday – Worship of all creation. Psalm 148

Saturday – Worthy is the Lamb. Revelation 5:6–14

Study Questions

1. How can we cultivate "holy expectancy"?

2. In the book I say that "God is actively seeking worshippers." Have you had any sense of God as the "Hound of Heaven" seeking you out and drawing you into fellowship and communion with Him?

3. The seventeenth-century Quaker theologian, Robert Barclay, spoke of the Quaker worship experience of being "gathered in the power of the Lord". He was obviously referring to more than the fact that they had come together in the same room. Discuss what the phrase might mean and once you agree on the meaning, consider what could be done to encourage a fuller sense of that experience in your local church.

4. What forms of worship have you experienced that have been especially meaningful to you? Do you have any sense of why these particular ones have been meaningful as opposed to any other form?

5. Critique my rather bold statement that the Bible does not bind us to any universal form (i.e. wineskin) of worship. Can you think of any worship forms that should be universally binding upon all cultures of Christians at all times?

6. What advantages or disadvantages do you see in the formalized liturgy used in churches like the Episcopal Church as opposed

to the more informal worship forms used in churches like the Southern Baptist Church?

7. If we truly believe that Christ is alive and present among His people in all His offices, what practical difference would that make in our approach to worship?

8. Do you think experiences of Divine ecstasy are central to worship, peripheral to worship, or destructive of worship?

9. What covenant can you make that will open the door to worship more effectively for you?

10. I write, "Just as worship begins in Holy Expectancy it ends in Holy Obedience." What does that mean for you for this next week?

Suggestions for Further Reading

Adams, Doug, *Congregational Dancing in Christian Worship*, Austin: The Sharing Co., 1971. (Gives a discussion of the history of dance in the Church.)

Emswiler, Thomas Neufer, and Sharon Neufer Emswiler, *Wholeness in Worship*, San Francisco: Harper & Row, Publishers, Inc., 1980. (Contemporary and practical. Hopefully it can bring fire to worship that is too rationalistic, and depth to worship that has focused upon feelings.)

Kelly, Thomas, *The Eternal Promise*, New York: Harper & Row, Publishers, Inc., 1966. (Kelly's essay "The Gathered Meeting" which is contained in this book is probably the most powerful Quaker statement on worship in the twentieth century.)

Nee, Watchman, *Assembling Together*, New York: Christian Fellowship Publishers, Inc., 1973. (Practical instruction in the life of worship.)

Steere, Douglas V., *Prayer and Worship*, New York: Association Press, 1940. (An intimate discussion of private and public worship by a contemporary giant on the devotional life.)

Underhill, Evelyn, *Worship*, Westport: Hyperion Press, 1980. (A standard by an important person among the devotional writers.)

White, James F., *Christian Worship in Transition*, Nashville: Abingdon, 1976. (Provides substantial historical and theological roots for worship.)

White, James F., *New Forms of Worship*, Nashville: Abingdon, 1971. (Practical guidance for those planning worship by one who teaches Christian worship at Perkins School of Theology.)

Chapter 12

THE DISCIPLINE OF GUIDANCE

Guidance is the most radical of the Disciplines because it goes to the heart of this matter of walking with God. Guidance means the glorious life of hearing God's voice and obeying His word.

The goal of guidance is not specific instructions about this or that matter but conformity to the image of Christ. Paul said, "Those whom he foreknew he also predestined to be conformed to the image of his Son" (Romans 8:29). Specific guidance in particular matters is a happy by-product of this goal having worked its way into our lives.

We make such a mystery out of the matter of the will of God. The surest sign that it is God's will for us to be where we are is that we are there! Now if we throw that away, we throw away the sovereignty of God over our lives. When we can come to the place where we understand that where we are is holy ground, we will begin to understand the meaning of guidance.

The will of God is discovered as we become acquainted with God, learn His ways, and become His friend. As we do this God will take us right where we are and produce in us the winsome fruit of "love, joy, peace, patience, kindness, goodness, faithfulness, gentleness, self-control" (Gal. 5:22–23). As the friendship grows, as the conformity grows, we will know instinctively what actions would please Him, what decisions would be in accord with His way. Just as our intimate knowledge of and love for our wife or husband guides us to decisions we know they would approve, so our inward fellowship gives an inward knowledge of the ways of God.

There are, of course, the outward tests of God's guidance such as Scripture, the Christian community, divine providence working through circumstance, and our own personal integrity. There are also the exceptional means of guidance such as fleeces, dreams, visions, signs and angels. It is important for us to remember that God will not lead us in ways that are contrary to His known will. The Spirit that inspired the Scripture will lead us in ways consistent with the Scripture. Our understanding of God's ways is shaped and tempered by His self-revelation to us in the Bible.

We must also remember that there is such a thing as supernatural guidance that is not divine guidance. John the Beloved warns us to "test the spirits to see whether they are of God" (I John 4:1). There are principalities and powers who wage war against the Kingdom of God, and they are both real and dangerous.

And so we are not to listen to every voice that comes our way but only the voice of the true Shepherd. But here is the wonder of it all, for as Jesus reminded us He is the Good Shepherd and His sheep know His voice (John 10:4). We walk in the light, we fulfil His commandments, we put on the mind of Christ and as we do we find the voice of the true Shepherd quite different from all impostors. While Satan may push and condemn, Christ draws and encourages, and it is His voice that we obey.

Daily Scripture Readings

Sunday   — The pole star of faith. Hebrews 11

Monday   — The guidance of Divine Providence. Genesis 24:1–21

Tuesday   – The guidance of justice and obedience. Isaiah
              1:17, 18–20

Wednesday – Led into all truth. Proverbs 3:5–6, John 14:6,
              16:13, Acts 10:1–35

Thursday   – Closed doors, open doors. Acts 16:6–10,
              II Corinthians 2:12

Friday   – Listening or resisting? Acts 21:8–14

Saturday   – The family likeness. Romans 8:14, 28–30

Study Questions

1. Is the idea of guidance as a *corporate* Discipline new or strange to
   you?

2. What do you think I mean by the term "the Apostolic Church of
   the Spirit"? (Note: I am trying to give a rather different twist to
   the old concept of "Apostolic Succession".)

3. Do you believe that this Spirit-led, Spirit-intoxicated, Spirit-
   empowered people have already been gathered, or are yet to be
   gathered in our century?

4. Do you think that the notion of a people under the direct
   theocratic rule of God is workable or is it only an illusory
   pipe-dream? Am I reading the history of the early Church
   through rose-coloured glasses?

5. In what sense does the contemporary charismatic movement
   approximate to or fall short of this vision of a gathered people of
   the Spirit?

6. What are some of the dangers of corporate guidance?

7. What do you understand the idea of a "spiritual director" to mean? Are there dangers to the idea? Are there advantages to the idea?

8. How should the idea of guidance influence the ways we carry on business in our churches? If we believed in guidance would it change our present church polity in any way?

9. Have you ever seen the idea of corporate guidance used in destructive ways? What lessons were you able to learn from that experience?

10. If living in guidance comes about mainly through entering into friendship with God so that we know and desire His ways, what should you drop from your life and what should you add to your life in order to deepen your intimacy with Christ?

Suggestions for Further Reading

Edwards, Tilden, *Spiritual Friend*, New York: Paulist Press, 1980. (Sensitive and sane counsel on reclaiming the gift of Spiritual Direction.)

Elliot, Elisabeth, *A Slow & Certain Light*, London: Pickering & Inglis Ltd., 1979. (A slender volume filled with meaningful and mature counsel.)

Leech, Kenneth, *Soul Friend*, London: Sheldon Press, 1977. (Provides a superb history of Spiritual Direction and links it to the best of contemporary psychology.)

Mumford, Bob, *Take Another Look At Guidance*, Plainfield: Logos International, 1971. (Wise and practical instruction from a leader in the charismatic movement.)

Nebe, August, *Luther as Spiritual Adviser*, trans. C.A. Hay and C.E. Hay, Philadelphia: 1894. (Helps us to understand Luther in the great tradition of Spiritual Directors.)

Smith, Blaine, M., *Knowing God's Will: Biblical Principles on Guidance*, London: Ark Publishing, 1980. (Helpful common sense counsel on guidance with an especially valuable section on the process of decision-making.)

St John of the Cross, *The Dark Night of the Soul*, London: Burns & Oates Ltd., 1976. (A classic on the spiritual life showing God's guidance and teaching in the experiences of hiddenness and stillness.)

Chapter 13

THE DISCIPLINE OF CELEBRATION

The Psalmist exclaimed, "Our mouth was filled with laughter, and our tongue with shouts of joy" (Ps. 126:2). And St Augustine echoed Scripture's words with the declaration, "A Christian should be an alleluia from head to foot." Celebration is a happy characteristic of those who walk cheerfully over the earth in the power of the Lord.

The joy of the Lord is not merely a good feeling. It is acquainted with suffering and sorrow, heartache and pain. It is not found by seeking it. It does not come by trying to pump up the right emotions, or by having a cheery disposition, or by attempting to be an optimist.

Joy is the result of provision, place and personality functioning properly in the course of our daily lives. It comes as a result of the abundant life Jesus promised having taken over the ingrained habit patterns of our lives. It slips in unawares as our attention is focused upon the Kingdom of God.

Joy makes us strong. I'll never forget the day I heard the words of Agnes Sanford, "On one of my most joyful and therefore most powerful days . . ." I do not remember the rest of the statement, but I never forgot the connection she made between joy and power. I have found this to be true, and I imagine you have also. On those days when the joy of the Lord seems to engulf us, there is an almost unhindered flow of God's life and power from us to others.

Celebration is a grace because it comes unmerited from the hand of God. It is also a Discipline because there is a work to be done. In Hebrews we are instructed to "continually offer up a sacrifice of praise to God, that is, the fruit of lips that acknowledge his name" (Heb. 13:15). The sacrifice of praise is the work to which we are called. In the Old Testament there was a morning and an evening sacrifice. That, I think, is a good beginning for all New Testament priests, of which you are one. Begin the day with the morning sacrifice of praise, "Lord, I love You, adore You, worship You, desire Your will and way . . ." Conclude the day with the evening sacrifice of thanksgiving, "Thank You, Lord, thank You for Your love, Your presence, Your strength and grace . . ." And as we do this the fire will fall upon the sacrifice of our lips just as it did upon the altar of old. God's joy will come, and there will be dance and song and joy unspeakable and full of glory.

Before long we will find ourselves taking a "thanksgiving" break rather than a coffee break at 10:00 and at 2:00. Soon so rich and full will be our experience that we will desire to be continually in His presence with thanksgiving in our hearts. And all of this will be occurring while we are carrying out the demands of our days – eating, working, playing, even sleeping. Belief in God turns into acquaintanceship and then into friendship. We look into the face of God until we ache with bliss, as Frank Laubach witnessed, "I know what it means to be 'God-intoxicated' ".

As noted before, this joy is beyond the pseudo gaiety of superficial religion. It is in no way connected with the "smile if you love Jesus" froth of today. It is not even necessarily tied to spiritual ecstasy. Its source is found in the assurance of being rooted and grounded in God. It is the experience known to all the saints and confessed by Brother Lawrence, "Lord, I am yours, dryness does not matter nor affect me!"

Daily Scripture Readings

Sunday — The Lord has triumphed gloriously. Exodus 15:1–2, 20–21

Monday — The joy of the Lord. II Samuel 6:12–19

Tuesday — Bless the Lord. Psalm 103

Wednesday — Praise the Lord. Psalm 150

Thursday — Hosanna! Luke 19:35–40, John 12:12–19

Friday — Walking and leaping and praising God. Acts 3:1–10

Saturday — Hallelujah! Revelation 19:1–8

Study Questions

1. Do you enjoy God?

2. There is a body of teaching which instructs us to praise God *for* all things, there is another which urges us to praise God *in* all things. Do you feel that the difference is significant and if so why?

3. Imagine some close friends in your church who have just received the news that their eight-year-old daughter has been killed in an automobile accident. Should your attitude with them be: "Weep with those who weep", or "Rejoice in the Lord always: again I say, rejoice"?

4. Why do you think a wholesome evening of side-splitting laughter with friends does you so much good?

5. Why do you think human beings often find celebration so difficult?

6. Which do you like better: spontaneous bursts of joy or planned expressions of celebration? Why?

7. If you are in a study group would you be willing to devise together some hearty holy shout and try it out together before dismissing the meeting?

8. How about planning out a family non-holiday celebration this year?

9. Do you find it easy to laugh at yourself?

10. At the close of this study what covenant *must* you make with the Lord?

Suggestions for Further Reading

Cornwall, Judson, *Let Us Praise*, Plainfield: Logos International, 1973. (A simple nuts and bolts book on the subject of praise in corporate worship.)

Howard, Thomas, *Chance or the Dance?*, Wheaton: Harold Shaw Publishers, 1969. (An engaging plea for the "old myth" of imagination and a devastating critique of the "new myth" of modern secularism.)

MacDougall, Bruce, *Rejoice in the Lord*, Nashville: Abingdon Press, 1978. (A celebration of all those "unexpected" changes in life that often cause confusion but can bring doxology.)

Reid, Clyde, *Celebrate the Temporary*, San Francisco: Harper & Row, Publishers, Inc., 1972. (A happy book about the author's personal pilgrimage and particularly his enounters with the human potential movement.)

Smith, Hannah Whitall, *The Christian's Secret of a Happy Life*, Westwood, Revell Company, 1952. (First published in 1870 it has become a genuine classic on the life of joy.)

Wainwright, Geoffrey, *Doxology: The Praise of God in Worship, Doctrine and Life*, London: Epworth Press, 1979. (The best modern work on the subject. In 609 pages Wainwright perceptively discusses Christian faith and life from the viewpoint of praise and worship.)

CELEBRATION OF DISCIPLINE

by

Richard Foster

'A stimulating guide for personal devotional life, and a source book for group study, prayer and worship. I warmly commend it.'

David Watson in his foreword

In this challenging study, the classical spiritual disciplines – meditation, prayer, study, simplicity, solitude, submission, service, confession, worship, guidance and celebration are given new relevance for today.

I BELIEVE IN THE CHURCH
STUDY GUIDE

by

David Watson

An invaluable companion to a radical and much-praised book.

Searching and practical questions on each chapter of I BELIEVE IN THE CHURCH are illustrated with the perceptive diagrams used by David Watson in his worldwide teaching. This Study Guide is ideal for individual and group study.

I BELIEVE IN THE CHURCH

by

David Watson

David Watson reveals the revolutionary potential of the family of God as he details the growth of St Michael-le-Belfrey in York from a handful of loyal attenders to a pioneering fellowship.

'He has seen a remarkable work grow under his hand.' *Michael Green*